FURLOUGHS,
FURLONGS,
AND
POTLUCK
DINNERS

1995-96 NWMS READING BOOKS

RESOURCE BOOK FOR THE LEADER

TOUCHING LIVES THROUGH SHARING
Edited by Beverlee Borbe

FOR THE READER

ARROWS OF THE ALMIGHTY
The Story of William Bromley,
Pioneer Missionary to Papua New Guinea
By A. A. E. Berg

FURLOUGHS, FURLONGS, AND POTLUCK DINNERS
Stories from the Deputation Trail
By A. Brent Cobb

MY LIFE AMONG THE NAVAJO
A Ministry to Body and Soul
By Beulah Campbell

RUN WITH THE TORCH
The Church of the Nazarene in El Salvador
By Eunice Bryant

BRINGING GOD'S WORD TO GUATEMALA
The Life and Work of William and Betty Sedat
By Lorraine O. Schultz

TREASURES IN THE DARKNESS
Stories from Behind Broken Walls
By Sharon R. Martin

FURLOUGHS, FURLONGS, *AND* POTLUCK DINNERS

STORIES FROM THE DEPUTATION TRAIL

A. BRENT COBB

Nazarene Publishing House
Kansas City, Missouri

ISBN 083-411-559X

Printed in the United States of America

Cover design: Crandall Vail and Ted Ferguson

Cartoons: Merril Bennett

All Scripture quotations not otherwise designated
are from the *Holy Bible, New International Version*®
(NIV®). Copyright © 1973, 1978, 1984 by International
Bible Society. Used by permission of Zondervan Publishing House. All rights reserved.

Scripture quotations marked KJV
are from the King James Version.

10   9   8   7   6   5   4   3   2   1

To
Daniel, Skyler, Sara Jennifer,
and Adam Benjamin,
who, along with their mother, light up my life
and extend grace to me.
You are my main mission in life.

ABOUT THE AUTHOR

Rev. A. Brent Cobb is the regional director for the Asia-Pacific Region of the Church of the Nazarene. He has also served the church as a pastor and as a missionary to Korea. Rev. Cobb, his wife, Marty, and their family currently make their home in Manila, Philippines.

CONTENTS

CONTENTS

PREFACE

Some of the funniest and most fascinating, frantic, challenging, and rewarding experiences missionaries ever have occur during their furloughs—their times of leave from their fields of service. I've long thought that furlough stories would make a captivating book. Others have said so as well.

I began interviewing missionaries to get their stories. Some of the "interviews," of course, had to be conducted by mail. I asked our missionaries to share vignettes about the other side of their service—in their homelands. Some of them are no-halo-type glimpses of not-so-glamorous incidents.

One example comes from a veteran missionary. Many years ago he was staying overnight in a Nazarene parsonage. In the night, when he tried to find the bathroom, he did not know which door to open. It was pitch dark. He thought he had the right door as he reached in to flip the light switch, but it was the master bedroom. Three fine people were left in a state of shock!

Many missionaries mentioned those wonderful missions potluck dinners. My wife, Marty, and I have been the "real, live missionaries" at many of these missions banquets. Nearly always, the head table has been positioned to face all the other people. We missionaries were honored by being made to go through the line first. As we did so, many fine cooks would come to point out their dishes, urging us not to pass up their specialties. Such food lines can be hard on missionaries' waistlines!

Then we would soon be made to sit at the center of the head table. We were usually told that the pastor and spouse would sit on one side of us, and the NWMS president and spouse on the other side. The pastor and NWMS president, however, generally would not go through the food line until everyone else had gone through. So the self-conscious missionaries had to sit there alone, facing many happy strangers eating a delicious meal.

Sometimes we would wonder if we would perhaps have gotten to know the people better if we'd simply been permitted to sit among them. At times it struck us that missionaries and typical Nazarenes at home must have quite different views, as symbolized by our sitting there facing different directions. I hope this little book will help us begin to hold a common view of what God has called us all to do.

There are lots of tremendous high and holy missionary deputation experiences. To relate some of these experiences is to put on display the beauty of holiness in the lives of God's people. Deputation services offer enormous benefits to local congregations.

Only eternity will reveal the influence missionaries doing deputation ministries have upon people in their homelands. Great blessing comes to churches when they minister to their missionaries and become involved in the work on the missionaries' field of labor. There are also benefits for the missionaries. Furloughs energize and equip missionaries for more effective service when they return to their adopted lands.

May you learn a lot as you read about missionary deputation. Enjoy your journey down the deputation trail.

Hearing the Call
(Kenneth and Joanna Schubert)

In was early in 1971. Ken and Joanna were pastoring a home mission congregation in Bakersfield, California. They learned that their church had been given the opportunity to host a missionary deputation service with Bill and Nancy Zumwalt. Following Nancy's long illness, which had delayed their preparation and departure, the Zumwalts were now ready to leave for Taiwan. This service would be a big event for their little congregation, Greenfield Church of the Nazarene (now known as Faith Church of the Nazarene).

The anticipated coming of the Zumwalts created tremendous excitement for the Schuberts. The two couples had been best friends in Kansas City. Both had attended Nazarene Theological Seminary at the same time and had served together at the Wornall Road Church of the Nazarene (now known as Summit View Church of the Nazarene) under the pastoral guidance of Dr. Kenneth Rice. And the Schuberts had become quite attached to little John Zumwalt.

It was a happy reunion when Bill, Nancy, and John arrived at the parsonage in Bakersfield that afternoon. "My, how John has grown!" exclaimed Joanna. Soon everyone seemed to be talking at once in an effort to get caught up on the news of the latest events. Everyone helped unload their things so that they could settle into the parsonage. They would spend the night there, but it was unlikely that they would get much sleep. There was so much to talk about and so little time.

Ken and Joanna could hardly wait to get through the suppertime so that they could help set up the projectors and curio tables for the evening service. They were anxious to share the Zumwalts and their call to missions with their church people.

In the evening service, Bill and Nancy told of the grace of God that had called them, healed her, and was now preparing the way for them to leave soon for their field of service. They wanted to get to Taiwan so they could plunge into study of the Chinese language. Their desire was to help train national leaders and workers.

The young pastor and wife beamed as they took it all in. They had been praying that God would call someone from their church to missionary service. Of course, they thought that it would be a child or a teenager. The Lord answered their prayers, but not the way they had expected.

The Zumwalts not only shared their joy but also issued a challenge for people to become personally involved in the world mission of the church. God began speaking to Pastor Ken Schubert. "Ken," He said clearly, "I want you to go."

After the service ended, Ken went to Joanna and told her what had happened. She laughed, her eyes filling with tears of joy. "I heard the call too!" she cried.

It was no small thing for Joanna to acknowledge God's call and to say yes to missionary service. She had grown up in a pastor's home in Indiana, somehow acquiring many myths and misconceptions about what it means to be a missionary. She had been terrified that God might ask her to leave the safety of her homeland to go live in a hut, contend with snakes and witch doctors, and be ill from jungle fever.

Now, remarkably, her fears were dispelled. She and Ken could not wait to get alone with the missionaries again. Back in the parsonage, they told their guests that God had called them to be missionaries.

"Praise the Lord!" Nancy exclaimed. "We've thought for a long time that He might call you. We see in you the gifts and graces for cross-cultural service."

What a confirmation this was! Bill led them in a prayer of commitment, asking the Lord to bless the Schuberts and to guide their steps through the coming months, perhaps years, of preparation.

After this time of prayer together, Ken and Joanna plied the Zumwalts with questions. They needed to know how to get started. Bill and Nancy were delighted to help put them in contact with the World Mission Division in Kansas City.

It now made sense to Ken that he had felt strangely compelled, while studying at Nazarene Theological Seminary, to take courses in missions and cultural anthropology. The principles he had learned from Dr. Paul Orjala would serve him well on the field.

Soon after the Zumwalts left, the Schuberts wrote to the World Mission Division office at Nazarene World Headquarters. They quickly heard back from Franklin Cook, assistant to E. S. Phillips, World Mission Division director. Before many weeks they spoke with both these men and were encouraged by their practical suggestions.

After a couple of years the Schuberts were brought together with the other missionary candidates. They all took a battery of tests to help determine their suitability for missionary service for the church. They filled out personality profiles, psychological inventories, and language aptitude questionnaires.

In January of 1974, the Schuberts met with Dr. Jerald Johnson, the new director of the World Mission Division. Soon afterward, they were appointed missionaries of the Church of the Nazarene and assigned to South Korea. God had called them, and the church would soon be sending them.

All that God had brought them through in the past, in addition to their 20 years of effective missionary service in Korea since then, testifies to the value of visits by Nazarene missionaries to churches in their homelands.

God is using Nazarene missionaries in more than 100 world areas. And He is also using them in deputation services to speak to people. Through missionary deputation services He is calling many more laborers into His service.

"Out of the Mouths of Babes"

(Jerald and Alice Johnson; Donald and Adeline Owens)

Jerald and Alice Johnson were the pioneer missionaries for the Church of the Nazarene in Germany. In 1964 they returned to their homeland for their first furlough. They had come home to be with Alice's mother, who was dying of cancer. It was a tough time for them when they left in August of 1964, aware they would not see Mom again in this world. In September she went to be with the Lord.

During that furlough they were invited to Oregon as missionary speakers for the District Family Camp. After one of the sessions, they were strolling along the path toward their cabin when, to their utter dismay, they saw their three-year-old daughter, Carla, doing something quite out of character for her. Obviously highly agitated, she was screaming and hurling stones at some of the other children.

The Johnsons could scarcely believe their eyes. They rushed to Carla and demanded to know what had possessed her that she should be so out of control. Tearfully, she replied, "They say I be missionary."

Dad and Mom fought back the impulse to burst into laughter when they recognized that little Carla did not have a clue what "missionary" meant. But she felt sure it must be something bad!

Today, Carla, the Johnsons' three-year-old, rock-throwing daughter, has grown up to answer God's call to missionary service. Now she can truly say, "I be missionary." She and her husband, Rev. Chuck Sunberg, are Nazarene missionaries to Russia along with their little daughters, Christa and Cara.

One fond memory Donald and Adeline Owens cherish comes from their first furlough. Their daughter Donna Jean was about two and a half years old. They were touring the Alabama District with Dr. and Mrs. L. S. Oliver. In all the deputation services Adeline wore her beautiful traditional Korean attire, and little Donna Jean wore her colorful Korean dress and komushin (rubber shoes).

Mrs. Bea Oliver had Adeline and Donna on the platform during the early part of each service. One evening, as they were singing "Send the Light," little Donna noticed that Mrs. Oliver did not have a hymnal. Donna was holding her own hymnal, though she could not read, so she politely handed hers to Mrs. Oliver, walked down off the platform to the front pew, and brought another songbook to the platform. She then proceeded to sing with great gusto, though the hymnal she was holding was upside down and opened to the wrong section. Amid the laughter of the congregation, Donna kept singing, making her joyful noise unto the Lord.

You Can Make a Difference

(William and Frances Vaughters)

It happened while they were on furlough in 1954. The church in Indiana was packed with enthusiastic Nazarenes gathered for a mission rally. Missionary Bill Vaughters was hoping to meet a Nazarene pastor and his wife who unknowingly had helped the work in Guatemala. He knew they lived somewhere in Indiana or Ohio, and he wanted to meet them. He wanted them to know that they had played a role in solving a major problem on the mission field.

Shortly after World War II, corrugated metal roofing was scarce in Guatemala. The walls of the new Nazarene church in Livingston had just been constructed, but no roofing material could be found. Bill learned, however, that the Guatemalan government was storing a supply of the corrugated roofing material at the customs building in the town where the Vaughterses lived. It was being kept for use on a government building near the docks.

Bill petitioned the officials to lend him enough roofing material to cover the church, promising to replace it with identical roofing, which was already being shipped to him from the United States. They refused to grant his request.

The rainy season was fast approaching, bringing downpours and flooding. With the church structure uncovered, Bill could foresee disaster ahead. The thought of an Alabaster-funded chapel being drenched and ruined by heavy rains sent him in desperation to Guatemala City. There he went directly to the National Palace.

He requested an appointment with the secretary of the treasury, praying that he might listen to his plea to authorize a loan of roofing material from the government supply stored in the customs building back in Livingston. He was informed that the secretary was away, but he would be allowed to speak with the undersecretary if he wished.

The missionary, of course, accepted the offer. He was ushered into a large, lavish office and introduced to the man sitting behind a splendid mahogany desk. They exchanged pleasantries. Then the man listened attentively as the young missionary made his request. Suddenly, when Bill mentioned the Church of the Nazarene, the official sat up and became animated with interest. He steered the conversation from roofing to people.

He told Bill that he had attended a state university in Ohio. In those days he had lived in the home of a pastor and his wife—Rev. and Mrs. R. L. Rich. They had treated him like a son. As he spoke fondly of those dear people, Bill's heart rejoiced to realize that something good was about to happen.

The influence of the Riches on a Guatemalan student became the basis for a government release of roofing materials to the Church of the Nazarene. Our church in Livingston was saved from ruin, and God was glorified.

So as Missionary Vaughters addressed the zone rally in Indiana, he told this story. In the service sat Pastor and Mrs. Rich, the godly couple Bill hoped to meet so he could thank them for their investment in the life of one Guatemalan student. A faithful, generous pastor and wife had "cast [their] bread upon the waters," and "after many days" it had come back in blessing for the Kingdom (Eccles. 11:1).

4 Reentry
(Hubert and Virginia Helling)

Taking the "High Road" Home

In 1963 General Superintendent G. B. Williamson wrote to Hubert and Virginia Helling in Japan. "Would you mind coming on furlough by way of Alaska and touring the district?" he asked. After prayer, they replied that they would be delighted to come through Alaska and speak in the churches there.

It was their first transpacific jet flight. They felt as though they were pressed into their seats when the plane took off. The kids were excited about the cold and snow they were anticipating in Alaska. A Nazarene military couple, the Bohalls, had provided coats for each of them.

To their surprise, they arrived in Alaska during a season of warm weather. The sun seemed to be working overtime as daylight hours continued into the night, until about one o'clock in the morning.

The Hellings were told that theirs was the first-ever missionary deputation tour on the Alaska District. Visiting the churches, they informed the people of what their dollars were doing in Japan. They could rejoice that their missions investments were already beginning to pay eternal dividends. In those days Alaska Nazarenes felt that they themselves were on a mission field. Now, however, they have become strong supporters of missions. Since 1979, the Alaska District has been self-supporting. Today there are many thriving Nazarene churches across that vast region.

When the Helling family made that first-ever tour of the Alaska District, transportation on the district was mostly by plane. The *Grummond Goose* and several other pontoon-equipped planes took the missionaries into the beautiful fjords where there were no highways.

The Helling family learned about permafrost, the big cabbages at Palmer, and the amazing blue glacial ice. Then there was Ketchikan, where the kids were delighted to catch a large cod almost every time they threw in a fishing line.

The Hellings were impressed by the devotion and drive they observed in Alaska Nazarenes. They found them to be true pioneers. That deputation tour was a tremendous delight both for them and for their new Alaskan friends.

Embarrassed in Their Home Church

Furloughs are mostly encouraging and ego-building times. But living in an oriental culture like that of Japan formed in the Hellings some hard-to-break habits. One of them worked to their disadvantage on their fourth furlough.

As usual, they had returned to Nampa, Idaho, for their furlough year. Nampa First Church had been their home church since college days. It had been tremendously supportive of the Hellings on the field as well as when they returned on furlough. The church's new sanctuary had just been completed, and the Hellings were attending their first Sunday morning worship service in the new building.

They were pleased to see a few of the old-timers among the many new worshipers, since they felt almost like strangers in their own home church. They sat on the front left side of the sanctuary, almost alone in that immediate area.

Following the organ prelude, the sanctuary grew quiet in anticipation of the first hymn. Hubert and Virginia stood to sing, as all Nazarenes in Japan do for the opening hymn. They had already sung two verses before they glanced around to discover that they were the only ones

standing in a congregation of well over 1,000 worshipers. They slowly sank to the seats, wishing they could sink through the floor as well.

No explanation could be given on the spot, of course. It was a few weeks later when Hubert Helling was beginning to address the crowd that he explained, "Of course we stood! We always stand for the first hymn in churches in Japan." Their field of service had left its mark on them.

Yes, missionaries can be different, all right. It may show up in strange accents and expressions in their speech, in bowing to a puzzled mail carrier, and occasionally in beginning to drive on the wrong side of the street. But their hearts are still like those of Nazarenes in their homeland— loving, caring, sincere, eager to share the joy of salvation with everyone in the whole world.

The differences come from their having been transplanted into a strange new culture. Eventually that culture loses its strangeness for them, and it becomes their very own. Indeed, for the Hellings, furloughs offered many tests in reentry adjustment to North American culture. But by the grace of God they passed them all.

The Final Long Furlough

How do missionaries know when to quit? Can they just close the door on decades of overseas service and stay home? When the Hellings were planning for furlough in 1979, the Japan District had become fully self-supporting. "Where do we go? What do we do now?" were questions they were asking themselves and asking the Lord.

After 27 years in Japan, they had 4 more years before retirement. They had always planned to stay in Japan until that time. But now they needed to know God's will for the rest of their ministry years. Were their dreams about to be dashed due to the healthy turn of events that led the Japan District to full self-reliance? Or did God have a special plan for them?

During a break in Hubert's busy deputation schedule, they drove to Abbotsford, British Columbia, to visit Chester and Vivian Mulder, former missionaries to Japan. Returning home by way of Seattle, the Hellings were immediately attracted to that city and the surrounding area. They wondered if perhaps God would lead them, upon retirement, to serve in Seattle and do evangelism among university students and businesspeople from Japan and other Asian lands.

While they were waiting for the Lord's answer, a letter arrived from a friend. They were heartened by the verse of Scripture that was included. "For I know the thoughts that I think toward you, saith the LORD, thoughts of peace, and not of evil, to give you an expected end" (Jer. 29:11, KJV).

Virginia had already been hearing the Lord speak to her from the words of Scripture that declare that "in quietness and in confidence shall be your strength" (Isa. 30:15, KJV). But what was the Lord planning?

The Hellings felt strangely drawn to work among the refugees and various ethnic groups in

Seattle. When they approached Dr. Kenneth Vogt, superintendent of the Washington Pacific District, he said that he also felt an urgency to reach internationals in the Puget Sound area. In 1981 the Hellings were delighted to learn that the mission board was appointing them to Seattle to do missionary work. Their assignment was to challenge the churches of western Washington to intensify their efforts to reach people of the many ethnic groups.

To seize this strategic opportunity, the Hellings visited and spoke to most of the congregations across the district. They also began to work with Washington Literacy and World Relief and lead a school in Seattle's Chinatown, teaching English and the Bible.

Virginia writes, "This assignment gave us work to do not merely for four years, but for as many years as we are able. We can stay right here. The work is all around us. There is no retiring! We love these people with whom we are working. The promise is true: 'Delight thyself also in the LORD; and he shall give thee the desires of thine heart' (Ps. 37:4, KJV)."

Author's note: It was my joy to have Rev. Hubert and Virginia Helling as my pastoral staff colleagues at Seattle First Church before I moved to Manila. They have now been serving the church and district for many years, and they are still going strong.

A Long and Winding Road

(Margaret Birchard)

It was the depression days in 1934. Russell and Margaret Birchard were under appointment, but they were told that they must raise funds for their own transportation and for their first year's salary if they wanted to get to Guatemala in the near future.

So the Birchards left their pastorate in Altoona, Pennsylvania. Traveling with their five-week-old daughter, Mary Margaret, their first stop was the district assembly at Pittsburgh. When they were introduced, their baby daughter elicited great affection from the gathered Nazarenes.

Leaving the district assembly, they traveled to a different church each night for a scheduled deputation service as they made their way to Michigan. Charged with the awesome task of raising enough money to live off of for a year, they were often given an evening offering that was only just enough to get them to their next place. (Imagine what it would be like to earn your salary that way!)

When the Birchards arrived in Michigan, they stayed with Russell's parents while they held services across the district and began collecting needed items for the field. Due to steep duty charges, no packages could be sent to our missionaries in Guatemala, so the missionaries already serving there asked the Birchards to bring them needed supplies, along with the Birchards' own things. Also, they had to take bandages, linens, and surgical equipment for the medical dispensary Margaret would set up and operate.

Eventually the Birchards were able to buy a four-wheel trailer on which they would load their trunks. Soon they were saying good-bye to loved ones and heading south.

While the Birchards were visiting relatives in South Carolina, the World Mission Department in Kansas City told them that a letter with tickets enclosed would await them in New Orleans. They cut their visit short in order to hurry on to New Orleans. When they arrived, they went to the steamship office to get their letter and tickets from headquarters.

No tickets were enclosed. The letter said, "Hold steady; your visas have not been granted." There they were—their trailer loaded with trunks, little money in their pockets, and stranded in a strange city where they knew no one!

After some searching, they succeeded in locating a garage to rent for storing their trailer. Then they "borrowed" the $8 that relatives had given to the baby, filled their gas tank, bought two hamburgers, and drove all night to get to Margaret's uncle's home. He was a Methodist minister in Selma, Alabama.

Checking on the visa problem, they learned that the Guatemalan government had a new law that blocked the coming of more Protestant missionaries but allowed replacements if some should leave the country. When the townspeople of Cobán, Guatemala, learned that the Birchards' visas had been denied, they decided to make a special appeal to the president of Guatemala. They said that since Margaret had been born in Cobán and wanted to return to the land of her birth to do much-needed medical work, she should be allowed in with her husband and their

infant daughter. The request was written as a formal petition with all the legal stamps affixed and was signed by some 150 petitioners.

The petition worked. Soon the Birchards were on their way back to New Orleans. When they arrived safely on the field, six-month-old Mary Margaret was adored by her maternal grandparents, the Richard Andersons, upon their seeing her for the first time. And Margaret was grateful to be "home" at last.

6

Loving Lord, Loving Nazarenes

(Norman and Carol Zurcher)

LINKS

The Woodland, California, Nazarenes invited Norman and Carol Zurcher to speak for their midyear mission conference. They were excited about getting to know their LINKS missionaries, and the Zurchers looked forward to being with these dear people, who had become like family to them through letters, cards, and gifts they had sent to them in the Republic of South Africa.

A wonderful chemistry began to bond them together during the Saturday evening international potluck dinner. The people were enthralled as they viewed the Zurchers' slides and heard them speak about their work.

The air was charged with excitement when Norman and Carol arrived at the church on Sunday morning. Hostesses helped them put on name tags with large gold stars. The tags read, "Starring Norman" and "Starring Carol."

It was planned that each Sunday School class would have its picture taken with the missionaries.

Everyone would receive his own picture the following Sunday. This allowed the missionaries to meet the members of every class, from the babies they held in the nursery to the senior citizens with whom they visited.

When it was time to enter the sanctuary for the morning service, they were escorted to a special spot on the front row. At a planned point in the service a plastic parrot on a perch descended from the ceiling and stopped just in front of the Zurchers. In the parrot's beak was an envelope marked "Special Delivery." A note written on the front instructed them to bring the envelope to the platform and to open it and read its message to everyone.

They read the following message:

This letter is to inform you that you are loved very dearly by the people here in the Woodland Church of the Nazarene. We pray for you and do our best to give you all the support we can. However, this letter is not just full of good wishes. We'll show you our love with a full set of dishes!

Just as they finished reading the letter, the doors at the back of the sanctuary swung open, and two men came carrying a table down the aisle and positioned it in front of everyone. Norman and Carol were told to approach the table. Displayed there was a full set of dishes and serving bowls in a pattern called "woodland brown."

For weeks before the missionaries' coming, a sign-up table had been in the foyer. It held a placard that read, "Buy Dishes for Our 'Adopted

Missionaries,' the Zurchers." Now, on this special Sunday morning, each piece was tagged with the name of the person or family who had provided it. A large bowl at the center of the table contained extra money given by everyone to help the missionaries buy a vacuum cleaner.

This was some 15 years ago. The Woodland Nazarenes have had other adopted missionaries since then. Yet when the Zurchers use their woodland brown dishes each day, they often recall their Woodland LINKS family, and their hearts are strangely warmed.

"LINKS," as you know, stands for *Loving, Interested Nazarenes Knowing and Sharing.* Certainly the Woodland Nazarenes held up their part of the human LINKS chain. From the opening international dinner to the closing Sunday evening sending service for their adopted missionaries, they dished out lots of love.

Separation

Separation is a way of life for missionaries. Even when they come home on furlough, they still may not spend much time with their families. When the Zurchers came to the United States for their sixth furlough, Carol decided not to accompany Norman on his first tour so that she could see their little grandsons, who had been born during their last term of service.

Carol's parents offered to drive her from Indiana to New York to visit Carol and Norman's oldest daughter, her husband, and the Zurchers' little grandson, Robbie. Robbie and his cousin Jarrod were the Zurchers' first grandchildren. Carol says, "I was full of grandmotherly excitement as we arrived at their parsonage home."

After hugs and kisses, Kay announced, "We have something to tell you: Just within the last hour, the doctor confirmed that we are going to have another baby! Mom, what are the chances of my being able to tell you our news in person and that you would be the very first one to know?"

They embraced and wept from the sheer joy of being together, being able to share those wonderful moments, having missed many such special moments in the past. Carol thought, How great that I can come and be with my daughter, as other moms do for their daughters, when she has her baby.

Then, remembering that this short furlough would soon slip by, Carol hesitatingly asked, "When is your due date?"

"That's the sad news," Kay replied. "It's five days after your departure date."

Carol and Norman were locked into a definite date to return to South Africa due to their having come home on a special round-the-world ticket that allowed them to stop in Papua New Guinea. There they had visited their other daughter, Janelle Fosnaugh, and her husband, Lane, who were also Nazarene missionaries. It would therefore be impossible for them to stay longer in the United States.

That night at her daughter's home in New York, when everyone had gone to bed, Carol cried and told the Lord that she was tired of separation from her family. She longed to be able to stay with Kay and other family members.

The Lord seemed to speak to her from Isa. 49:23, assuring her, "Those who hope in me will not be disappointed." She wanted to believe that promise, but in the matter of separation from family, she realized that it would fully apply only when she and Norman retire or when they get to heaven.

At breakfast the next morning, Kay searched her mug collection for a suitable one in which to serve her mother coffee. It was a Precious Moments mug with the words "Praise the Lord Anyhow!"

A short time later Carol noticed a church sign-board with this statement: "When faithfulness is most difficult, it is most necessary." Carol's response was to say yes again to God's will for her life—even though it would mean more separation.

A couple of months later, Norman and Carol were doing deputation work together in California. When they arrived one evening for supper before a service, the pastor said, "Your daughter in New York has been trying to reach you. She wants you to call her."

Carol's first thought was that Kay must have lost her baby; when she reached her daughter by phone, she discovered her intuition was correct. Mother wept with daughter as they talked over the long-distance phone lines. Carol grieved that though she was in the United States for furlough, still she was separated from Kay by thousands of miles.

The Lord gave Carol two verses during the remaining months of furlough—scriptures that challenged her to return to South Africa for their seventh term of service. They were these:

Now finish the work, so that your eager willingness to do it may be matched by your completion of it, according to your means (2 Cor. 8:11).

You need to persevere so that when you have done the will of God, you will receive what he has promised. For in just a very little while, "He who is coming will come and will not delay. But my righteous one will live by faith. And if he shrinks back, I will not be pleased with him." But we are not of those who shrink back (Heb. 10:36-39).

The Lord knew that Carol would need these verses back in Africa upon learning that they were to become grandparents again and again and again. That news came to them three more times in five months during their first year back on the field.

Though Carol missed being present for her grandchildren's births, she thanks the Lord for photos and videotapes, which will enable them to know their grandchildren when they first see them on their next furlough. By that time the children will be almost four years of age.

Cartoons and Consecration

(Merril Bennett; Fred Huff)

Those who know Merril Bennett know about his sense of humor. It has found expression in his cartoons, done under the pen name Abe, which have appeared in several publications and can be found scattered throughout this book.

Merril always illustrated his deputation messages with a series of cartoons drawn on newsprint with charcoal or chalk. One time he was

42

at a church for a conference lasting several days and drew his pictures as part of his presentation. After one service an influential member told him, "I hope you'll have more meat in the message tomorrow night."

"I thought about drawing a cow," Merril says, "but I restrained myself."

That member's comment put the missionary under bondage, but after praying about the matter, he felt he should continue his cartooning. He did, but he also did some extra praying.

The final service, on a Sunday evening, was a high time. When the missionary gave an invitation, young people lined the altar, bowing in surrender to God's call for their lives.

He may have imagined it, but it seemed to Merril that the person who had critically commented on the first service now had a look of astonishment on her face. Certainly, the responsiveness of the people was not due to the missionary's greatness but to God's grace.

Fred Huff is another missionary God has used to speak to young people. On one occasion he was the missionary speaker at a Nazarene camp for boys and girls. He was given an hour each morning and evening to tell the children about missions. Fred also enjoyed getting close to the kids during the other activities of the camp.

On the last night of the camp the main speaker gave an invitation. He instructed those who sensed God speaking to them about missionary service to meet the missionary at the altar. Thirteen boys and girls responded. Missionary Huff took them out of the tabernacle and into a church bus, where they sat to talk and pray together.

An 11-year-old boy told them that he liked "playing missionary." Sometimes, however, his friends would say, "We don't want to play that missionary game; you play it by yourself." But he did not mind, because he knew the Lord had called him to be a missionary. He looked forward to answering the divine call.

Later, at a teen camp in South Carolina, Fred Huff again had the privilege of praying with young people God was calling to mission service. The highlight of Fred's furlough experiences was being able to see young people respond to God's call to serve Him across national, cultural, and linguistic barriers.

New Missionaries, Old Friends

(Robert and Colleen Skinner)

Colleen Skinner grew up in the Philippines, where her parents, Dr. and Mrs. Ronald Beech, served as Nazarene missionaries. Bob Skinner grew up in Oregon and went to Boise State University in Idaho. He was a football star who seemed destined for a professional sports career, but God had other plans.

God's will for Bob and Colleen involved not only marriage but also master's degrees for both of them. They earned them at Nazarene Theological Seminary as part of their preparation for missionary service. That preparation also included special service in the Philippines prior to their full appointment as Nazarene missionaries.

Bob pondered what his main message should be during his three months of deputation services before their departure. Though he knew an abundance of information to share with people about the Philippines, the Lord seemed to lead him to tell how he had come to be a missionary.

He felt he should speak to people not as a missionary with a bit of experience already under his belt, but as one of them—a regular person, opening his heart to people among whom he had lived. He needed to tell them what it was like to receive God's guidance, even when that divine direction pointed to missionary service.

As new appointees, the Skinners scheduled their own deputation services. One of their first services was at the Meridian Valley Shepherd Church of the Nazarene in Idaho, where Bob had served for three years as youth pastor.

They were thrilled to be back home on that Sunday evening. The people were excited, and the fellowship was sweet. Bob spoke with conviction about God's call for his life. He underscored the fact that the Lord deals with each of us uniquely and personally. Then he ended with a challenge to the people. He told them to ask, "Lord, what are You saying to me?"

Then Colleen came to sing "Take My Life, and Let It Be Consecrated." It was supposed to be a closing prayer; but when she concluded, the pastor sensed the Holy Spirit's leading to open the altar. Quickly the altar became lined with young people who had been in the youth group Bob had previously led. Adults also came forward to pray.

Conviction was so strong and the Spirit's work was so real in the church that other scheduled events were affected. A dessert fellowship time and baby shower for the missionaries' newborn son was delayed so long that many people had to go on home, straight from the glow of God's manifested presence. Bob, Colleen, and the others knew that something was happening that was more important than eating cake and ice cream or opening baby presents.

God had greatly used the Skinners' deputation ministry. Everyone had been in the presence of God. Many had experienced His transforming grace. Some had heard God's call and offered themselves to go in His name.

An Answered Prayer
(John and Doris Anderson)

During their 1976 furlough, John and Doris Anderson received a unique answer to a prayer they had prayed back in India. Believing they would be assigned to urban ministry next term, they asked the Lord to provide a "small piano"—adding, "if one exists." Actually, they had never seen or heard of such a piano. But they knew it would be out of the question for them to take back a large piano with a full keyboard. Shipping costs, customs fees, and limited floor space in India made a smaller piano a necessity.

Bob and Pat Highfield, friends of John and Doris in Howell, Michigan, offered to loan them their motor home. So the four Andersons drove it to the General Assembly in Dallas. Doris was scheduled for surgery in Chicago the following week, but John was scheduled to speak at a camp in Pennsylvania. Their first thought was to cancel John's appointment, but the Lord seemed to tell them both that John should go on to Pennsylvania in the motor home.

Since the Highfields were keeping the car the Andersons would be driving for the rest of the furlough year, John planned to return from Pennsylvania to get the car and then meet his family in Chicago. Their home church would take good care of them until he got there.

At the camp in Pennsylvania, John worked with a team of musicians composed of two generations of the Bender family, who included him in some of their special music. As the camp was concluding, the Benders announced their desire to give the piano they had brought with them "for the work in India."

It was a peculiar piano, however, since its keyboard had two fewer octaves than normal. What jubilation there was at the camp when John told them about his prayers for such a piano—"if one exists"!

They loaded the piano into the motor home, and John transported it to Mount Vernon, Ohio, where the Andersons would live during their furlough. Then he returned the motor home and went to be with his family.

A sequel to this story occurred on the Bombay docks when, more than a year later, their sea freight arrived. A customs official asked to see their import license, something they did not know they needed.

Since John could not produce a license, the official said he would at least have to prove that someone in the family could play the instrument. So the missionary sat on the piano bench in the customs storehouse and began to sing and play "Jesus Is Lord of All." A clear Christian testimony went forth, and the piano quickly cleared customs with a duty charge of less than $20.

Pontiac in the Pond

(Stephen Rieder)

It was a wet day in May 1983. Steve Rieder, then a missionary to Taiwan, was home on furlough. That day he was driving through the rain from one deputation service to another. As he came around a curve, he noticed a sign that warned of water in the road ahead. The thought flashed through his mind: If there's water in the road often enough to have a permanent warning sign, why not put in a drain to take care of the problem?

He saw water across the road near the railroad underpass. It looked to be only an inch or two deep, so he slowed down. When he got closer, however, he realized the water was deeper than he had thought, but it was too late to stop. The white Pontiac Phoenix began to hydroplane out of control. Steve cried out, "Lord, help me!"

It seemed to him that the Lord's strong hand nudged the car over to the left side. An oncoming car grazed the right back side of Steve's car before that Pontiac) left the road in a flying leap and landed in a three-foot-deep pond. The missionary wasted no time getting free of his seat belt, rolling down a window, and slithering through it to get on top of the car. He was barely able to jump to the bank.

Soon Steve was bemoaning the fact that he had not had the presence of mind to remove his missions display, projection equipment, and clothes from the car. The driver of the other car came running to see if she could help, and Steve was relieved to learn that no one had been hurt. The police came and issued him a $50 citation; then a wrecker arrived to haul off the missionary's car with its soaked curios, projector, slides, and personal effects.

To make matters worse, Steve had just come from Michigan, where he had been given a supply of soap and other items for use on the mission field. Everything was soaked.

But Steve Rieder soon was viewing the incident as an occasion for rejoicing and thanking God. He had escaped injury because the car had not flipped over and landed on its roof, which would have made it harder to climb out to safety. The driver of the other car, though she was not wearing a seat belt and had received a bump on her forehead, was OK. Steve was also thankful for good comprehensive insurance coverage.

Missionary Rieder writes:

> There I was in a strange town, and I needed help. So I went to the phone book. I have lots of good friends in the Baptist, Presbyterian, and Pentecostal churches. But that day I passed over all those church names. I looked for "Church of the Nazarene." There it was. I called Rev. Charles Bugbee of Watseka [Illinois].

The gracious pastor came to help. He found a repair garage for the waterlogged vehicle and then invited Steve to spread out his wet things to dry in several rooms of the parsonage, where he provided lodging for the grateful missionary.

The next day Pastor Bugbee transported Steve all the way to Olivet Nazarene College (now Olivet Nazarene University). A little later, on another district, Superintendent Dr. Tom Hermon loaned the missionary a plush Chrysler New Yorker to drive for a month until his car was ready to go again.

God's wonderful people in the Church of the Nazarene pulled Stephen Rieder out of his trouble and set him on a dry, solid rock (a concrete highway!), sending him on his way rejoicing.

Giving Living

(Glenn and Ruth Irwin; Paul and Nettie Stroud)

It is amazing how much a personal connection can do to encourage the missionary vision of a church. When Glenn and Ruth Irwin came on furlough from Papua New Guinea, they learned that their home church had paid all its budgets for the first time in years so that their missionaries would not be ashamed of them. They also handed the Irwins a love offering that was enough to cover an unexpected rent deposit on the house in which they would be living during furlough.

On another furlough the Irwins were part of a Nazarene church in a different area of the country. Their involvement in the church stimulated the people to greater giving. That year they overpaid the church's budgets by 15 percent.

The generous spirit of the Irwins affected the people they were around. Glowing reports came back to Dr. Irwin from other missionaries about the impression he had made on pastors' families with whom he had stayed. They admired the way he acted like a "real" person, even helping with the dishes after meals.

The Irwins recall their tight finances during their first furlough, when Glenn was doing further studies at a university. They went out most weekends for missions services, but sometimes their expenses were nearly as great as the offerings. When they wondered if there would be enough for the next week's groceries, someone in a service would give them a "$20 handshake." Glenn observes, "Interestingly enough, during subsequent furloughs, when funds were not so tight, there were no more $20 handshakes."

One of the most trying times for Glenn and Ruth was when they left behind a married daughter who still had to "pray through" about

Mom and Dad going back to the field. Episodes leading up to this prayer caused pain for the missionary parents. They wondered why her letters were so out of character for their normally sweet, loving daughter.

Thank God, she did pray through, and so did her parents. It's hard for missionary kids to give up having grandparents for their kids. Returning to the field also tests the grandparents' devotion. It makes their hearts heavy to leave growing grandchildren, knowing they will miss many special moments of their childhood.

But the Irwins say the same thing that many of our other missionaries around the world say— that it pays to serve Christ and His Church as missionaries. God grants compensations that are more than commensurate with the sacrifices they and their families must make.

Paul and Nettie Stroud also experienced Nazarene generosity in unexpected ways. The place was Noblesville, Indiana. Paul and Nettie arrived at the lovely church building and were met by some gracious members. They helped the missionaries carry in their exhibit and projection equipment, but the missionaries could sense that something strange was in the air that evening.

The deputation service had a strained ambience. The mood was melancholy. Paul and Nettie sensed the tension on the faces and in the voices of the people. It seems that the pastor, after years of fruitful ministry, had just resigned and was moving to another pastorate. The devoted church members were still in shock.

The Strouds did their very best in the mission presentation that evening. Then, as the service was drawing to a close, someone asked, "How much does one of the accordions that you need in Cape Verde cost?" "About $400," was Paul's response. Within a few moments the people gave enough for an accordion, plus a generous offering for the missionaries' own equipment needs.

Paul and Nettie were astonished. They gave glory to God that the seeds they had sown that night—though they expected little in return—had fallen onto good ground. God was glorified in all the people who were present—in the departing, godly pastor; in the missionaries who were passing through; and in the mission-minded Nazarene laypeople who were remaining.

Homecoming Highlights
(Daniel and Melody Anderson)

Before they left for Kenya in 1986, the Anderson family had to adjust to having Daddy gone from the home during his many trips. Four-year-old Becky especially had a difficult time with his leaving.

One cold winter morning Dan was leaving early for another deputation tour. Little Becky heard him and followed him outside. Still in her nightgown, and with tears streaming down her face, she peered into the car window. The missionary did not realize she was there until he heard her anguished words, "Daddy, don't you love me anymore?"

Still, in spite of the difficulties, the Andersons made it through that first deputation tour. Four years later, they arrived home for their first furlough. As they stepped from the plane at the Sacramento Airport, the Andersons' first glimpse of family and friends was tinted yellow: everyone in the large crowd was waving big, yellow ribbons that said, "Welcome Home!"

Several months before their furlough, Dan had communicated with his father that he needed him to find a car for them to use while they were on furlough. They had discussed the cost, gas mileage, size, make, model, year, and many other considerations.

Dan's father plied him with questions as soon as they got away from the airport and had time to talk. "Son, what kind of car did you say you want? How much money can you pay? What kind of gas mileage does it have to get? And when did you need it?"

By then, Dan's mom spoke up: "Oh, Bud, just tell him!" And he did.

It seems a Nazarene couple had recently moved to Auburn, California, and united with the church. They had decided to buy a new car. Then they asked the pastor if he knew of a missionary family that needed a car. They would just give them their old car.

This is how it happened that during their furlough year the Andersons drove a 1979 Cadillac. God had again shown them that He was well able to supply all their needs.

In their home church the Andersons got to spend time with their good missionary friends, Dr. Bill and Marsha McCoy and family. They were home from Swaziland, and the two families' furloughs overlapped for six months. At the Sacramento District NWMS Convention, President Bev Borbe had the Andersons and McCoys come to the platform, along with their parents and other relatives. Then she asked the throng of people to give a "stadium cheer" to show their love and support for their district missionaries.

What a cheer! What clapping! It seemed to go on and on. The two missionary families will not soon forget the chanting: "Go! Go! Go! Go! Go! . . ."

Danny Anderson was only two years old when he left the United States to go with his family to Kenya. Most of his Sundays were spent in rural Kenyan churches. On his first Sunday back in their home church in California, six-year-old Danny asked his mama about the altar. Since there are no altars in the bush churches, Danny wanted to know why the people were praying at that "rail thing" at the front of the sanctuary. Melody explained "family open-altar time."

Little Danny said, "Well, I've already asked Jesus into my heart, but I just like to talk with God. Can I go too, Mama?"

You can be sure that "Missionary Mama" was pleased to kneel beside her son at that wonderful, sacred place Nazarenes call the altar.

Tough Times, Tremendous Times

(Timothy and Mary Mercer)

A difficult furlough time for Mary Mercer came when she was quite ill and not sure what was the cause of the illness. Week after week, she had to watch her husband, Tim, walk out the door to go on another deputation tour.

Mary testifies that even these tough times were growing times for her. During Tim's absences she came to understand something of the loneliness and hardship that single parents go through as they have to bear heavy responsibilities alone. Mary has learned what it's like to make decisions without having a spouse present to use as a sounding board. Now she can empathize better with singles at couple-oriented church social events.

Best of all, Mary can now testify that the Lord will never leave nor forsake His own. He is with His children when they go through the valley as well as when they are on the mountaintop.

The Mercers have enjoyed a number of enriching times while on furlough. Rather than merely citing one or two examples of furlough highlights, Tim and Mary offer the following short list of joys:

1. Watching churches go beyond their goals during Faith Promise Conventions in which they spoke

2. Meeting Nazarenes all across their homeland and hearing them say, "I've been praying for you"

3. Sharing with young people who are sensing a call to mission service

4. Getting to know new Christians who are awakening to the excitement of mission involvement

5. "Stocking up" on family get-togethers over cups of tea

6. Meeting a special relative for lunch

7. Sending a daughter off to the mission field on a Work and Witness trip made possible by prayed-in money given by an elderly prayer warrior, widow of a Nazarene pastor

8. Seeing another daughter receive Christian baptism in the church of which they had been a part during their furlough year and hearing her give her first public testimony

Ecstasies and Agonies
(Brent and Marty Cobb)

First Church of the Nazarene of Henderson, Kentucky, made furloughs fun for our family. The people gave us poundings and showers to provide us with clothes, toys, food, and spending money.

The thing I appreciated most came in 1979, at the beginning of second furlough. Our church sent me to Haiti as part of a Kentucky District Work and Witness team. It was a joy to help complete the construction of a simple chapel and then attend the dedication service with Dr. Charles Strickland preaching. A throng of more than 1,300 happy Haitian Nazarenes jammed the new building.

Pisgah Community Church on the Southwestern Ohio District was extravagant in its gift giving to us. As part of a Sunday morning deputation service, a boy came down the aisle riding a new Huffy bike for eight-year-old Danny. Then a girl came down the other aisle on a Hot Wheels for three-year-old Sara.

Our kids beamed to see the Lord provide the "dream gift" each had wanted most. Danny was a bit disturbed a few days later, however, when a motorist in a restaurant parking lot hit his new bike, ruining a wheel. But when we got to the next church, the pastor had a replacement wheel for him, and Danny learned that nothing is too hard for the Lord.

Soon after we had arrived home for our second furlough, Irmgard Williams, our pastor's wife, had a surprise for Marty. She took Marty to a factory outlet store in Evansville, Indiana. Three hours later they returned and displayed Marty's six new dresses.

A short time later we were in Old Hickory, Tennessee. It was a special treat to visit in the home of Jim, Brenda, and little Mary Beth Agee. We had become friends in Korea when Jim had a tour of military duty there. We stayed with them several days while having deputation services in the Nashville area. One day Jim invited me to his workshop to help him make a rocking cradle for Sara's doll. It was Sara's third birthday, and she was elated with her custom-crafted gift. In addition to this, the Agees took us all to Opryland.

In spite of such wonderful times as these, we had a few less-than-pleasant incidents as well. On one occasion we failed to allow enough time for travel. It was nearly midnight on Saturday when we rolled into Indianapolis. We were tired, and we took the first motel we found. We did not think about the fact that the sign in front advertised "Day Rates."

The room was dirty, and sirens blared all night. Something seemed strange about the motel and the surrounding area. When we mentioned this to folks at the Nazarene church on Sunday morning, they asked the name of the motel. Hearing our reply, they burst into laughter. We had been in the red-light district, in its most notorious motel.

Another not-so-glamorous aspect of our second furlough was the used motor home in which we traveled on longer trips. On our first trip the holding tank cracked. The embarrassing leakage prompted me to crawl on my back under the motor home to try to repair the problem. Rain was pouring down.

My first effort at repair made matters worse. The crack widened, and I got drenched. The smell was horrendous. I did not feel very holy, but I certainly felt humbled. With the help of my brother-in-law, we finally got the problem solved. But a short time later we had a new challenge—a leaking gas tank.

Fiberglass patches failed. So too did my resolve not to fret. Could things get worse? We got our answer to that question while traveling along a rural road in south Texas. One of the two steel bands supporting the gas tank broke, and the 40-gallon container began to drag against the road surface.

By the mercies of God we were able to stop quickly before a spark ignited the gasoline. Soon the Lord sent us an "angel of mercy" to make repairs, and we rushed off to our deputation service in Houston.

Our most frightening experience with the motor home came from its faulty furnace. The first time we really needed to use the furnace was after we drove over the Tehachapi Pass in California. It was late at night when we located the Nazarene church and parked in front to get some sleep.

The temperature was below freezing. We turned the dial on the thermostat to start the propane furnace. There was a strange hissing sound like that of escaping gas. I immediately turned off the furnace.

Over the protests of the others, I refused to use the furnace and risk all our lives. I knew the heating chamber could quickly fill with gas. Then the electronic ignition would spark a blaze that could consume us in flames or blow us away in one great explosion.

We later thanked God for protecting us and keeping us from freezing as we huddled close through that long night. The next day I discovered the problem: the gas flow control unit we had just paid to have replaced had been installed backward.

Near the end of our first furlough, I spoke in my childhood church—Lexington, Kentucky, First Church. After I concluded my message, Pastor Riley Laymon gave an invitation. Our six-and-a-half-year-old son, Stevie, stepped out and went forward publicly to trust Jesus Christ as his Savior. It happened at the very altar and spot where I had been converted at the same age.

No one would have dreamed that within five weeks, after having returned to Korea, we would experience a tragedy that would claim Stevie's life. But when that happened we felt the loving support of Nazarenes worldwide.

We thank God for the prayers of thousands of people in our time of loss and sorrow. When life dealt us its worst, we saw God's people at their best. We are grateful too for a denomination and mission board that brought us back home briefly to experience the loving care of family and church friends.

Missionary furloughs and deputation services can be double blessings. They serve to remind those of us who are missionaries that we are not on our own. We are supported by a great denominational family of people who pay, who pray, who obey, and who care. In addition to this, furloughs and deputation services give us the opportunity to extend our ministry, allowing us to touch the lives of thousands of people in our homelands.

APPENDIX

How You Can Contribute to a Successful Deputation Service

What is involved in a successful deputation service? There are seven steps to take to assure success: prayer, preparation, planning, publicity, promotion, provision, and opportunity.

Prayer

The pastor and the council members of a local church's Nazarene World Mission Society should pray for guidance in seeking to secure a missionary speaker for deputation services. After the date is set and a missionary is scheduled, everyone should pray for the missionary, the missionary's family, and the missionary's field of service. Not only does prayer make a difference for the missionary, but also God uses it to heighten interest in missions in the local church. You begin to care for those for whom you pray.

Preparation

Missionary deputation services are far more effective when all the people of the church are mentally and spiritually prepared to identify

with the missionary. One goal of deputation work is that the people in the local church shall come to view the missionary as their representative. He or she is sent by them to carry out the "uttermost part of the earth" dimension of their involvement in the Great Commission (Acts 1:8, KJV). They will therefore want to help their missionary representative in God's work by their prayers and financial support.

Planning

If you are one of those who helps to plan the deputation service, be sure to make that a priority. Plan the events of the weekend and the order of the service so the congregation can focus on missions and not be distracted by other things. Be sure the missionary has adequate time to tell his or her story well.

If you are not part of the actual planning of the service and events, be sure you make yourself aware of what is going on. Reserve extra events for some other time. Get to know the missionary in a personal way so that you may continue to have a genuine interest in the missionary and in the work on the field he or she represents even after the deputation service is over.

Publicity

The local church leaders should have someone contact the deputation coordinator in the World Mission Division office to request a news release and photo of the missionary. Not only are these useful for publicity within the local congregation through the church newsletter and bulletin board, but also they may be released to local newspapers. Flyers may be handed out by believers to their friends and distributed in the neighborhood.

Everyone in the church should review the missionary books or *World Mission* articles about the missionary and the field. Learn where the field is, what language is spoken there, and what the climate and traditional religions of the area are like. This will enable you to be informed in advance and will give you a greater appreciation for the missionary and the missionary's work.

Promotion

Leaders in the church can maximize the value of a missionary's coming by beginning to generate excitement about the event weeks or even months ahead of the set date. Worship leaders should give opportunities for skits and brief news notes during services. Sunday School classes and small groups should also present sound bites to promote the coming missionary service.

Provision

The missionary is your ambassador and should be treated as such. If you can, volunteer to assist the missionary with a trip to the Laundromat, post office, or wherever he or she may need to go. Do all you can to encourage and be a blessing to the missionary.

Missionaries carry back to their fields fond memories of the fellowship and helpfulness they experienced in local churches in their homelands. Make a missionary's visit an uplifting time—an occasion to build his or her faith and morale.

Opportunity

The missionary deputation service provides you a golden opportunity. It will challenge children, young people, and adults to commit their lives to Christ and to seek to discover and do God's will for them. One of the highest callings anyone can receive and follow is the call to serve Christ on the mission field. Be open to what the Lord may say to you during the deputation service.

Another Key Point

Boosting the deputation offering is a key way for a church or district to be a blessing to a visiting missionary. Beyond covering the missionary's travel costs, a generous offering will help with other furlough expenses. Additionally, the missionary uses the deputation offerings for equipment that makes his or her field work more effective. Often deputation funds are needed to purchase an automobile or other such large item. At times, in addition to the deputation offering, special giving by the church or by individuals will fund Approved Special projects for the missionary's field of service.

These are just some of the things you can do to get ready for a wonderful time of ministry, but the list is by no means exhaustive. Be creative in what you do to prepare yourself and your family both to be blessed and to be a blessing. Include prayers for missionaries in your family devotions. Do something special that will really make the missionary feel at home in your church. Remember that this is another chance to make a difference in the life of a missionary and in the kingdom of God around the world. Whatever you do, don't waste the opportunity.